Cultural Celebrations

EASTER

by Elizabeth Andrews

WELCOME TO DiscoverRoo!

This book is filled with videos, puzzles, games, and more! Scan the QR codes* while you read, or visit the website below to make this book pop.

popbooksonline.com/easter

abdobooks.com

Published by Pop!, a division of ABDO, PO Box 398166, Minneapolis, Minnesota 55439. Copyright © 2024 by Abdo Consulting Group, Inc. International copyrights reserved in all countries. No part of this book may be reproduced in any form without written permission from the publisher. DiscoverRoo™ is a trademark and logo of Pop!.

Printed in the United States of America, North Mankato, Minnesota.

102023
012024

THIS BOOK CONTAINS RECYCLED MATERIALS

Cover Photo: Shutterstock Images
Interior Photos: Shutterstock Images; Getty Images
Editor: Emily Dreher
Series Designer: Colleen McLaren

Library of Congress Control Number: 2023939062

Publisher's Cataloging-in-Publication Data
Names: Andrews, Elizabeth, author.
Title: Easter / by Elizabeth Andrews
Description: Minneapolis, Minnesota : Pop!, 2024 | Series: Cultural celebrations | Includes online resources and index
Identifiers: ISBN 9781098245375 (lib. bdg.) | ISBN 9781098245931 (ebook)
Subjects: LCSH: Easter--Juvenile literature. | Eastertide--Juvenile literature. | Religious festivals--Juvenile literature. | Holidays--Juvenile literature. | Cultural sociology--Juvenile literature.
Classification: DDC 394.26--dc23

*Scanning QR codes requires a web-enabled smart device with a QR code reader app and a camera.

TABLE OF CONTENTS

CHAPTER 1
Bunnies and Baskets 4

CHAPTER 2
History of Easter 8

CHAPTER 3
Easter Season 14

CHAPTER 4
Easter Around the World 22

Making Connections. 30
Glossary 31
Index. 32
Online Resources 32

CHAPTER 1
BUNNIES AND BASKETS

Anna woke up early on Sunday morning. She got out of bed and met her brother in the hallway. It was a bright spring day, and they were both excited. Their mom called out and told them it was okay to come downstairs and start the hunt. It was Easter!

WATCH A VIDEO HERE!

People get creative when dyeing Easter eggs. The eggs can have different patterns.

Anna and her brother each found six dyed eggs hidden around the house. They also spotted their Easter baskets. The baskets were filled with candy and a special toy. The Easter Bunny had been to their house!

Easter chocolate comes in many shapes and sizes.

Easter meals often include breakfast foods.

Before they could eat all the candy in their baskets, Anna and her brother had to get ready for church. She put on an Easter hat because she knew her grandma liked them. After church, they would go to her aunt's home for a delicious brunch with all their cousins. It was going to be a happy day.

CHAPTER 2

HISTORY OF EASTER

Easter is a Christian holiday that celebrates the resurrection, or rising from the dead, of Jesus Christ. The story of Jesus is the basis of Christianity. Christians believe that Jesus is the son of God. He died to make sure his followers could go to Heaven. When he came back from the dead, it proved how powerful God was.

LEARN MORE HERE!

Jesus was born to a woman named Mary.

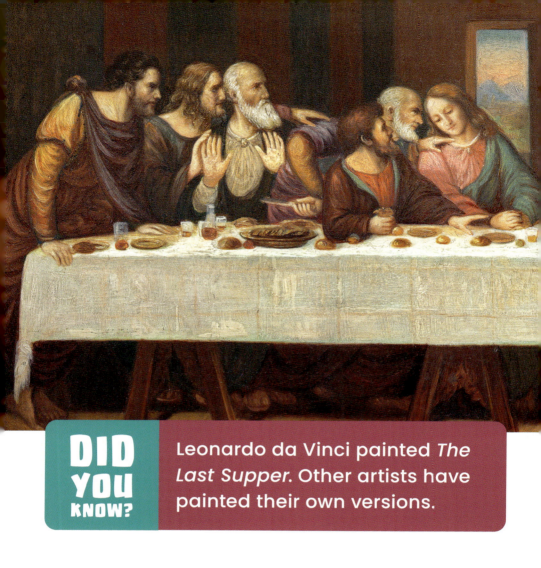

DID YOU KNOW? Leonardo da Vinci painted *The Last Supper*. Other artists have painted their own versions.

Jesus knew that he was going to die. It was what God planned for him since before he was born. The night before he

At the Last Supper, Jesus gave his apostles bread to represent his body and wine to represent his blood.

was arrested and punished with death, he held a supper. At the supper he told his **apostles** that he would die the next day. This meal is called the Last Supper.

Jesus was **crucified** by the Roman government. His family, friends, and followers were sad. They sat and guarded the **tomb** he was buried in for two days. On the third day, Jesus was resurrected. This means he rose from the dead. All the people who loved him were happy. His resurrection is celebrated every year on Easter.

Christians decorate with crosses. When a statue of Jesus is on a cross, it is called a crucifix.

Easter decorations are often pastel colored. Pastel colors are soft and pale.

Events that happen around Easter often match stories about Jesus from the **Bible**. However, some people celebrate Easter without going to religious ceremonies. Many children who are not Christian still get visits from the Easter Bunny. They may dye eggs just for fun!

CHAPTER 3

EASTER SEASON

There are several important days that happen during the week before Easter. This week is called Holy Week. Starting with Palm Sunday, Christians celebrate Jesus's return to the holy city of Jerusalem. In church on Palm Sunday, Christians are blessed and share palm branches.

EXPLORE LINKS HERE!

In a Bible story, townspeople laid cloaks and palm branches on the streets before Jesus.

DID YOU KNOW? Jesus did many good things in his life. He treated all people with kindness and love.

Jesus washed his apostles' feet during the Last Supper. It showed he loved and respected them.

Holy Thursday follows. It **honors** Jesus's Last Supper. Some Christians go to church the Thursday before Easter. They hear the story about the Last Supper and have **communion**. Some people may have their feet washed by their religious leader.

Good Friday is the day that Jesus died. It is a day of prayer and **mourning** for Christians. They honor Jesus's **sacrifice** to save them by attending church and hearing the story of his death. Some churches take down the decorations and quiet their bells.

LENT

Lent is a 40-day period when Christians prepare for Easter. It begins on a day called Ash Wednesday. People **fast** and avoid joyful things to honor Jesus. Some people don't eat meat on Fridays during Lent.

Christians believe that Jesus will return to Earth to judge the living and the dead.

HOLY WEEK

PALM SUNDAY: Jesus arrived in Jerusalem. People attend church and get palm leaves.

HOLY THURSDAY: Jesus held the Last Supper. People go to church and get their feet washed.

Saturday is the final day before Easter celebrations. Some people attend church services that last all through the

GOOD FRIDAY: Jesus was **crucified**. People attend church and hear the story of his death.

EASTER SUNDAY: Jesus rose from the dead. People celebrate with joyful traditions.

SATURDAY: Jesus's body was in the tomb. People attend church between sunset on Saturday and sunrise on Sunday.

night. These services represent the long period of time that Jesus's followers waited outside his **tomb**.

Some people get together with their extended family for church on Easter.

Easter Sunday is the main event. It is a time of joyous celebration! On Sunday morning Christians around the world attend church services. There they pray, sing songs, and receive communion. People often dress in nice, light-colored clothes. Sometimes women wear fancy hats.

Sunday is also the day that the Easter Bunny leaves baskets and eggs at people's homes. In the days before Easter, children and their friends and family dye eggs. Eggs symbolize new life, like the new life Jesus got upon his resurrection.

WHY EGGS?

Decorating eggs became a tradition when the Christian church told followers not to eat eggs between Palm Sunday and Easter Sunday. Since eggs were still being laid, people chose to use them as decoration.

CHAPTER 4

EASTER AROUND THE WORLD

Christians around the world celebrate Easter and its Holy Week in different and beautiful ways. In Guatemala, the town of Antigua covers the streets in bright, colorful carpets called *alfombras*. In 24 hours, people create the carpets out

COMPLETE AN ACTIVITY HERE!

of flowers, colored sand and sawdust, fruits, and vegetables. A procession walks along the carpets on Good Friday.

A procession usually includes a large group of people walking in one direction.

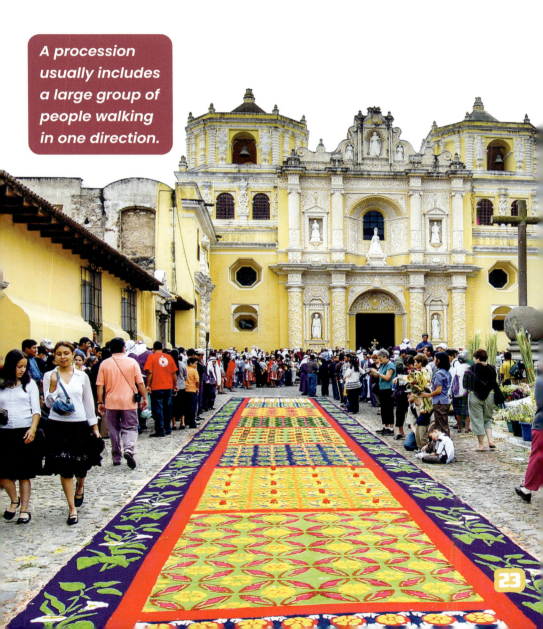

In Italy, Holy Week has very old traditions still being practiced today. Sicily hosts a Good Friday procession that includes 2,000 people. It is watched by more than 20,000 people. Hooded church members walk through town. They carry statues of Jesus and his mother, Mary. Church members and the people watching are sad as they **honor** Jesus's death.

The procession in Sicily is totally silent.

In Ethiopia, Christians celebrate Easter later than people in western cultures. *Fasika* is a 55-day period of **fasting** to honor Jesus's **sacrifice** and resurrection. They do not eat meat or dairy. On the night before Easter, they attend a long church service that lasts until morning. The following night, there is a large celebration full of food, dancing, and family.

Ethiopian fasting food usually includes flatbread, beans, and sauces.

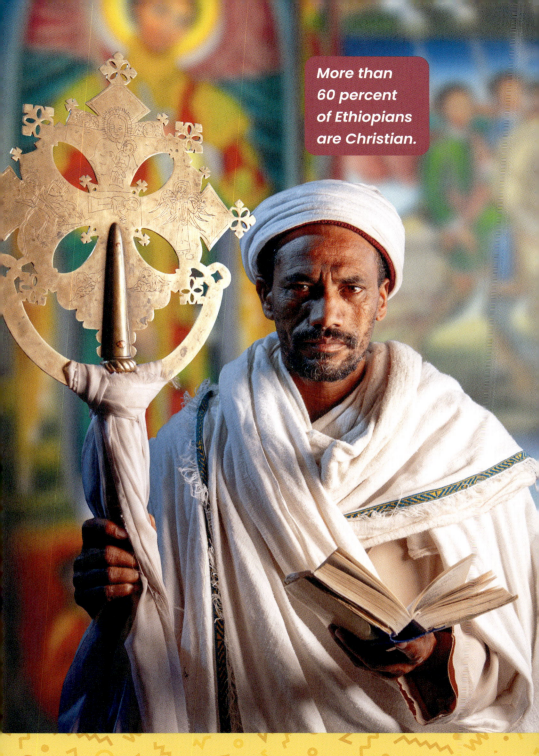

More than 60 percent of Ethiopians are Christian.

Most schools have the day off on Easter Monday.

A famous American Easter tradition is the White House Easter Egg Roll. It began in 1878 when Rutherford B. Hayes was president. On Easter Monday, children and their friends and family push eggs across the White House lawn. The goal is to roll an egg the farthest without it cracking.

Easter is a time to celebrate new life and the resurrection of Jesus! Family and friends make sure to spend time together. Many people who are not Christian choose to celebrate the Easter season because the traditions are fun and joyful.

Bunnies are associated with Easter because babies are born around the holiday.

MAKING CONNECTIONS

TEXT-TO-SELF

What Easter tradition were you most interested in? Have you ever taken part in the tradition? If so, did you enjoy it? If not, why are you interested?

TEXT-TO-TEXT

Have you read a book about any other Christian holidays? If so, how were they similar to and different from Easter?

TEXT-TO-WORLD

What global Easter celebration mentioned in this book were you most interested in? With help from an adult, look up a different country's celebration. Write a short paragraph describing the celebration.

GLOSSARY

apostle — one of Jesus's chosen 12 special followers. They continued to spread his teachings after he died and went to heaven.

Bible — a book including the Old and New Testaments believed to be given to humans by God.

communion — a Christian tradition where blessed bread and wine are consumed.

crucify — to be killed by having the hands and feet nailed to a cross.

fast — to purposefully not eat or drink.

honor — to regard with great respect.

mourn — to feel and express deep sadness.

sacrifice — the act of giving up something for the sake of helping others.

tomb — a place where a dead person is buried.

INDEX

baskets, 6–7

Bible, 13

church, 7, 14, 16–20, 25–26

crucifixion, 12, 19

Easter Bunny, 6, 13, 21

Easter Sunday, 19, 20–21

eggs, 6, 13, 21, 28

Ethiopia, 26

Good Friday, 17, 19, 23, 25

God, 8, 10

Guatemala, 22–23

Holy Thursday, 16, 18

Holy Week, 14, 16–21, 22, 25

Italy, 25

Jesus, 8, 10–13, 14, 16–17, 19, 21, 25–26, 29

Last Supper, 11, 16, 18

Palm Sunday, 14, 18

resurrection, 8, 12, 19, 21, 26, 29

United States, 28

This book is filled with videos, puzzles, games, and more! Scan the QR codes* while you read, or visit the website below to make this book pop.

popbooksonline.com/easter

*Scanning QR codes requires a web-enabled smart device with a QR code reader app and a camera.